FAITH, HOPE AND LOVE

...but the greatest of these is love

poetry by Heidi Frederick

And now these three remain: faith, hope, and love
But the greatest of these is love.
                    (1 Corinthians 13:13 NIV)

DEDICATION

This book is dedicated to those who, by faith, never lose hope by believing in the power of God's love.

"Poetry is the revelation of a feeling that the poet believes to be interior and personal, but which the reader recognizes as his own."
Salvatore Quasimodo

"Love is friendship set on Fire."
French proverb, author unknown

"What do we have if we don't have hope?"
Heidi Frederick

FAITH, HOPE, AND LOVE

...but the greatest of these is love

poetry by Heidi Frederick

TABLE OF CONTENTS

Trusting in God

PULL ME THROUGH

Holiness upon me
The world a different place
I gave myself to you
Gave up the hectic pace

I pray my Lord for guidance
In what you'd have me do
Just pull me through to glory Lord
To the life planned out by you.

I have visions
I have dreams
I know you'll take me there
Just let me lose myself in you
Cast away my cares

The tenderness and warmth
The knowledge and the truth
Have set me free, your steadfast love
I know will pull me through.

MORNING LIGHT

As I wake in the morning
And thank you for the day
My vision and my purpose
Looking upward all the way.

The dreams that occupy my heart
I prayed and asked for truth
Are no coincidence or myth
are heaven-sent by you.

I close my eyes and see a time
Of love so deep and true
I'll be a loving, giving wife
A Godly wife for you.

The creator of the universe
He chose this plan for us
Turned our paths and footsteps
When all we saw was dust.

He lifted us from sadness
A life grasping for truth
One day we'll stand together
With the innocence of youth.

Declare our love and trust
in our God above.
Conqueror of all despair
Thru His grace and love.

DEAR FATHER

Dear Father,

My heart aches for a love
so true, sometimes it hurts
and makes me blue.

It's then I pray and reach for you,
the only one pure through and through.

And once again I feel whole,
just knowing the wait is worth it all.
The bride of a man of God,
my wedding planned
before my life began.

Love,

Your Daughter

ALAS, WE MEET AGAIN

Thoughts of you
So warm and true
A wonderment
of things so new

From deep within
you fill the void
your voice to me
a joyful noise

Let I be for you, and let
You be for me
under His great love
what will be will be

I trust Him
with my heart and soul
He'll show us what
He has in store
Our God, our King
Forevermore.

ALL THINGS

You have led me to this day.
I trust in you, for you want the best for me.

As I approach the destination of change,
the stars twinkle like my eyes
when I think of you.
I enter the building and know you are there.
All at once, I am filled with peace
and the pounding of an overflowing,
hopeful heart.

I know not what lies ahead of me
but I look to you to guide me
by my faith, hope, and love.

My season for singing has come.
As you fill my heart, I will spill the love on
others, they will see the Holy Spirit before them,
through me.

Be with me today, Oh Lord, my comforter, my
friend, my protector,
you know my heart, you've listened
to my longing prayers.
You have not brought me this far
to disappoint me.

I know you will blow my mind with the miracle
of love and the transformation
of this life I've known.

God's Amazing Promises

INSPIRE ME TO DREAM

It's not that I deserve it
But Lord, it's my desire
To live a life of joy and peace
To touch and to inspire

To use these blessed gifts you gave
In a way that pleases you
That glorifies your Holy Name
to those who never knew.

Reveal to me each day
That dreams really do come true
for those of us who seek your face
delight ourselves in you.

The desires of my heart
Are so pure and run so deep
I know your promise that if I sow,
I too will surely reap.

I'm in awe of all your power
the love you have for me
May I live a life that pleases you
Full of joy and victory.

Do You Know?

Do you know…

How I count the days until I see you again?

How I search for your face in the crowd?

How I pray for your heart and soul?

*How I ask God to show me who you are
and why you are on my heart?*

*How I hope for the chance for my light
to give you warmth?*

*How ridiculously impossible the odds were
We would ever meet and yet we did?*

*Do you know that nothing is
impossible with God?*

A SECOND CHANCE

I can't put into words
The new realm in which I live
The Spirit is upon me
As I receive my daily bread

At times I look at the world
And all of its despair
I pray for God's protection
I know He sends me there.

He chose this time and place for me
To dwell upon the earth
The appointed time and gifts He gave
To show the lost what they are worth
Even the most wretched can be saved
If they simply seek new birth

Jesus can and will
His promises hold true
For the words I speak
Are from my heart
What He did for me,
He'll do for you.

SWEET PROMISES

The promises you make me
Of the love just down the road
Just thrill me and excite me, Lord
In all the ways you've told.

Everywhere I turn
You make your presence known
you assure me every single day
I am your very own.

Until that sweet day comes
when my love can be revealed,
when I can share with him, my love
exactly how I feel.

It rises deep inside me
It swells within my heart
I know the day is coming soon,
When we'll no longer be apart.

HIS PROMISE

*Your heart will show through your
eyes and you will be as one.*

*I will not forsake you,
trust in me and I will take you there.
Love me and he will love you.
Do not be afraid, for you are my child
and I love you.*

*Reach out and let him know.
You have been patient and will be richly
rewarded.*

MY LIGHT, MY HOPE

The balmy sky fills the air
like the fullness of my heart

The sea rolls in and out
like so many people in my life

The waves come and go, but the ocean is forever

The flicker of lightning
shoots across the sky
as if to surge my heart with new life
the hope and promise of things to come.

Timing

HIS TIME

Once again the path laid down
Our destinies collide
Here we are face to face
My love I cannot hide
I prayerfully seek a chance
to be right by your side.

Everything I've prayed for
is coming to the light
I must believe He's shown me you
for He knows my heart is right.

Whenever I am near you
or hear your blessed voice,
with all my heart and soul I pray,
He's revealing to me, His choice.

The one I'm meant to care for,
To support and share a life,
to show you tenderness and warmth
to be your loving wife.

You

I see the pain and sadness in your eyes
They tell a story of hurt and lies
the deep regrets, I sympathize,
my heart aches for you,
for you I cry.

I will be here for you today
May all your tomorrows be brighter,
I pray.
For you and I could share someday,
A love that never fades away.

My heart skips a beat
for my new found friend,
How I just know,
It's not the end.

There seemed to be
a planted seed,
two kindred souls,
both in need.

Our lives began in the same way,
For many years we felt betrayed,
by the ones who turned us away,
rejected, yet blessed in God's own way.
He knew the path we were to take
One day many years away,

The two would meet and sparks would fly,
Two gentle souls, yet filled with fire,
You are the one, my heart's desire.

The Author of romance now guides our days,
let no man stand in the way
He loves us both, we turn to Him,
our lives, a love story to begin.

A TIME FOR HARVEST

*Trust in the Lord to reveal the time of Harvest
For even when you think the fruit is ready to be
picked, only He knows when it is at its sweetest.*

*For fruit picked too early may look good to the
eye, but may be bitter or bland.
Let the fruit ripen on the vine
until it is ever so sweet.*

*Now my friends, take heart, learn to hear from
Him, for when He tells you it is time for Harvest,
You must trust Him and go to the field
to pick the fruit,*

*For if you hesitate,
the fruit may fall from the vine and spoil.
Which one of us wants to miss our chance
to enjoy God's perfect fruit for us.*

*Do not doubt that your seed has been planted.
The creator of Heaven and Earth is cultivating
him especially for you.
He wants to nourish your heart with the sweetest
fruit of all, His perfect choice to quench your
heart's thirsty desire.*

*Remember too, flourish in this time
that He has set aside to cleanse your palate*

so all bitter fruit of the past
may be washed away to allow you a fresh taste
of what He has always intended for you.

For such a time like this, is a precious
opportunity to feed your hungry soul.

STEPPING STONES

First love, so innocent and true
full of hope, raw and fooled,
rushed in too fast, lost in you.

Searched again, found a place, not so right,
no true embrace. Hanging on by a raveled thread
my heart grew cold, hunger not fed.
Pain and lies, I close my eyes
and years slipped quickly by.
I endured the pain, head held high, a part
of me had died inside.

A turning point, a new love grew
right in my womb, a blessing from you.
A chance for love, unconditional and true.
I build my life to raise you right,
you're my pride and joy,
my innocent and loving boy.

More years pass by, life on my own, another
chance, a stepping stone.
a driven one with lofty goals,
I try again for one to hold.
A good friend, so comfortable,
like a well worn shoe,
yet in the end, a shoe with no soul,
no word of truth.
You dismiss me back into the chilly world,

the tension builds, I cry out for someone to hold.
At long last, I find the one who I can trust,
who has my heart, knows my thoughts
warms my soul and bridges the gap.
He fills me with a knowing glow
that never again will I be alone.
He prepares my path, my heart, my soul, He gives
me strength to go
down the road, a narrow one
toward one true goal.
This time as I seek and find, He'll open the door,
in His due time.
Never again will I search on my own, let the
Spirit guide me,
My, how I have grown.

The stones of the past were built on sand.
Take me to a solid rock who holds
true to your commands
built on faith, truth and love.
Is filled with the Spirit from the one above.
Without you, we would never meet
but with your guidance, my life will be complete.

I look to you with eager eyes, full of hope and a
heart that cries
for patience as the one arrives.
The season of change is here. You have my heart,
I've nothing to fear.
You take my hand and lead me to
the one created for me by you.
All I had to do was ask, seek, and knock for a
love so true.

THE CALL

Days and nights passed quickly by
Empty words spoken on the fly
Days turned to years, my life incomplete
Waiting for something beyond my reach

I searched for it in hollow eyes,
declaring love not justified
Our souls connect, but not by God
I am left so unsatisfied,
I search for answers and find only lies

The division comes, the union dissolves,
unanswered questions, no resolve
The phone goes dead, my love has stalled
and that is when I received the call.

The Lord is near, He comforts my soul
and dries my tears.
He mends my heart, lifts my spirit high.
The love I feel I cannot deny
The day that I received His call
was the day I rose above it all.
My darkest fears, insecurities, have been laid to
rest, never to reappear.
My Lord has blessed me with a brand new life,
never again will I dwell in strife.
My life began with His loving call and He will
guide me through it all.

I now no longer see, the sad lost girl
I resolved to be.
The light of the Spirit now shines through me
and I have God's promise for eternity.

Waiting on the Lord

WINDOWS OF MY SOUL

*As the night falls
the day reaches its end
Once again, you come to mind*

*I stare out the window
and wonder
where are you,
what are you doing?*

*I sit in a room
filled with chatter
yet I drift off and dream
of the next time
we will meet*

*I know
I am certain
just not sure when or where*

*God delights in surprising us
When I least expect it
He will move suddenly!*

MOMENTS

Some moments in time, we did share
I pray the Lord revealed
Made you aware
Of the light in me
how much I care

Beyond all understanding
spirit led and true
my heart reaches out
yet I wait on Him for you

Few do understand me
as I wait so patiently
for the love I'm certain is on the way
He asks me just to be

He wants me to be joyous
in everything I do
and one day when all hope seems lost
He'll suddenly show me you

This way He gets the glory
nothing I could do
would lead me to my one true love
the blessing that is you.

WHILE I WAIT

My heart belongs to you,
I'll wait patiently, I'll be true.

I knew you were out there somehow, some way
And how I long for that sweet day.

When I can say right from my heart,
I had a notion from the start.
Well before I knew your name,
I prayed for you and saw that face.

I reflect on days gone by,
had always wondered when and why.

Now I know he had me wait,
Took me past those empty days

The change began a year ago,
when I first opened my heart and soul
To love the way, the truth, the life,
victorious and bold, I'll fight the fight.

We'll bond together as man and wife,
we'll save the world, one soul at a time
We'll make this world a better place,
by sharing the Word from His loving Grace.

TAKE TWO

This time no stranger's first hello.
A familiar face, a heart a soul.
A different place, a lot of noise,
will time stand still
our thoughts devoid
of what His perfect plan might be,
a friendship, a bond for eternity.

I'll be patient, I will wait
for all good things must bloom in faith.
In hope and truth, I seek again,
is this the beginning or the end?

God has a perfect plan for me,
I pray for strength beyond my reach.
I need you Lord, for all my days,
In every way, I give you praise.

THE WAIT

His eyes are like daggers,
Piercing my heart.
His smile is vulnerable
His face is unique,
like no one I've seen.

I wanted to hold him,
but resisted the urge,
afraid to mislead him.

My feelings are true and
from the heart,
yet I know he would find it
hard to fathom.

IF YOU ONLY KNEW

*My nature is of truth, yet I must
withhold from you for now.
I was drawn to you for reasons I cannot explain.
I knew little of you, but yearned to know more.
I believe God guided me to your path.*

*I wish you could know the warmth
I felt sitting by your side,
the tears I nearly cried as you embraced me
and I reached for you.
The things I wanted to say, but
knew it was not time.
For how could these feelings be
understood or explained.
You know our God and the
mysterious ways He works.
It is a wonder to me.
I want you to know what you do does not matter
but who you are does.*

*The way you looked into my eyes as
we spoke shook my soul.
I'm certain you have no idea what I felt inside.
I don't know where your heart is at
and I have no right to ask,
I just want you to remember me
and that I may be in your thoughts,
a snapshot in your memory.*

I believe you are a romantic,
intense, and passionate man.
Together with Him, we could
conquer this world.
How great it would be if God's plan
was to bond us in some way.

I will be patient. God will speak to my heart
and let me know if and when it is time.
The door has been opened and
I believe there is more to come.

Keep creating, keep dreaming, keep being true.
I see the beauty that lies within you,
more than you know.

Guidance

PRAISE HIM

Be with me, child, all your days
I will show you miraculous ways
I simply ask, just give me praise
Glorify me with your hands raised

Worship me with all your heart
For I have set you far apart
You've been chosen, you've been called
To serve the Most High, Lord of all

I'll be there, don't ever doubt
I'll never leave or turn away
When you are lost
have gone astray
I'll send my angels
To guide your way

I promise you through all your days
through valleys and trials
You will be raised
Just seek my face and give me praise.

TAKE ME AWAY

Take me to a land of truth
Where love abounds and I seek only you
I surrender to you my heart and soul
to purify me and make me whole.

The Spirit fills all hidden gaps
I'm sealed and full, there is no lack
For you fulfill my every need
simply written in your decree

I feel your presence in me ignite
the warmth spins me round with joy and delight
For you are truth, grace, and love
all pure gifts from above

Let me always seek you first
to guide my path. To know my worth
I'll not give up, will persevere
it's all I know, you're always near

The bumps will come, you'll see me through
You have been there by my side
I know it now, scales fallen from my eyes
no longer blind.

My dearest friend, trusted Father,
faithful provider, my strong tower,
my comforter, my strength, my shelter,
my guide....
My example of how I'm to live this life.

To My Father

*As I pray to my Loving Father
To guide me toward you,
He provides reassurance
through a shooting star.*

*My heart is so full,
it rumbles like thunder
aching to reveal itself.*

*My hope lies in my Father,
My Lord and the Holy Spirit
who has ignited a flame inside me
that I thought had extinguished long ago.*

*I have been washed clean
by the blood of my Savior
and bathed in Holy Water.*

*With the loving guidance of
my Heavenly Father,
I pray my light will shine brighter every day
and He will guide me toward my purpose
and unspeakable joy.*

THE LONG ROAD

The road won't be easy
But I will be strong
I won't settle
For anything less
Than His best.
I've waited so long,
It's bound to be true
for God has guided me to the
one and only you.

Experiencing True Love

To My Love,
My Heart's Desire

I have yet to meet you,
but know you are just a moment away.
You are a part of me, yet still apart from me
I long for the day when by God's loving grace,
our separate destinies will collide
and our lives will be intertwined forever.
I yearn to gaze into your soul-filled eyes,
to share myself with you.

My heart and soul tell me the time is near,
the search is drawing to a sweet demise.
A life of lost dreams, heartbreaking goodbyes,
unanswered questions will soon be washed away
through my everlasting faith, hope and love.

I've longed for the day when
I can hold you close,
our souls surge together as one
and I can finally proclaim I have found you,
my one true love.

I see you from across the room.
Is it really you?
Do I dare approach you?
Do I dare not?
Our eyes meet and I know the wait is over...
it is you.

THE MOMENT

The curtain rises, the lights grow dim,
the music begins, only moments 'til I see him.
The anticipation grown deep in my heart
finally hits the breaking point,
from here we start.

I see the eyes, the smile, and then the voice.
My heart is warm with its rejoice.
You are just as I pictured, yet not the same.
I long to hear you say my name.
You look like a child with joy in those eyes,
yet the presence of you is handsome and wise.

As the curtain closes, I am sad for its end,
But my heart tells me, this is where it begins
My heart beats with excitement
for possibilities of when.

Just as I'd dreamed many nights before,
I see you from across the crowded room.
My heart pounds , the warmth almost
overcomes me.
My mind races with what to do.
Do I dare approach you, do I dare not?

At the final moment, He takes my hand
and guides me toward you.
I can't explain why I am so drawn to you.
Someone I do not know, except for his song,

just needing to know so much more,
to someday talk all through the night.
My heart tells me we have so much to share.

SPECIAL K AND OJ

What a way to start my day
with Special K and sweet OJ
Please pass the smelling salts
for I think you are losing me
and winning me all at once

The sweet fruit that passes my lips
is not nearly as sweet
as the song in my heart
The loving serving is too much to digest

And you wonder why,
you act like you don't know
but the gleam in your eye
Is all I need to show

Coffee, tea or will you take me
will we soar on high
or cruise the sea
warm sandy beaches
cool ocean breezes

Let us move in unison
parallels that dare to touch
and break the rules of reason
Apart becomes a part of me
You and I ... He writes the story.
Let the music play,
the dance begin

Take my hand
we will learn the steps as we go
we'll spin and swerve
trip and sway
but we'll find our way

Our moves, our rhythm the perfect beat
You can dress me up and take me out
wine and dine me
but just promise me
the warmth of a home with you
that is all I really need

THE PROVERBIAL WIFE

My heart aches for you
This longing is far greater than
anything of the flesh
To know you will be the start of my journey
as the loving wife I was born to be.

I pray that God has waited so I will be prepared
with a gentle yet determined heart
full of love, hope, and endurance.

Will you join me on this walk
toward our loving Father
who loves us even more than we love each other?

God's Love Manifested

REFLECTIONS

When I reflect on days gone by
I catch a glimpse, you by my side
Times I know you carried me
when I felt trapped
you set me free

So many times, I felt so lost
The choices made, no prayerful thought
Ignorant of what it cost
You gave your life just for me
Your steadfast love
that set me free

You saw in me a flicker of hope
a tiny fire deep in my soul
you knew I'd come to seek the flame
you'd make me whole, you'd call my name

Your beloved one, who tried to cope
Relied on flesh, and had lost hope
Now knows the answer is your love
Turns to you, wisdom from above
The peace and joy burns deep inside
excitement I have in sharing this ride
This gift called life, I do embrace

By God's loving mercy and grace
I'm here for you
I'll go great lengths
Give up my ways
Give it all to you
The one who saved me
and taught me truth

GRACE

One time so brokenhearted
Lost and all alone
You reached down from Heaven
called me as your own

I never really knew you
but believed that you were there
I had no understanding
how very much you cared

You knew me long before
you placed me in my mother's womb
your plans for me so awesome
I just had to make some room

Now I know you're present
in everything I do
I search for ways to live my life
so righteous and so true

Today I thank you, Father
as you take me by the hand
your love shines through in every way
On your Word I stand

SURROUNDED

Lord, I love to feel your presence
when I smile or when I weep,
I feel you gazing down on me
the tear wiped from my cheek

Your love, it so engulfs me
like a blazing, holy fire,
you are the one who loves me best,
I am your heart's desire

Your love assures me of my worth,
whenever I may doubt,
when you come to fill me up,
I float upon the clouds

I start to feel the love rush in
as thick and sweet as honey,
I know the richness of His love
is more valuable than money

All things that I have gathered,
the possessions that I own,
pale in comparison
to the gifts sent from His throne.

He's called me out of loneliness, pain,
and such unrest,
because He loves me tenderly,
unconditionally, and best.

I proudly wear the crown,
the inheritance I accept,
use me Lord to spread the truth
to let someone know they're next.

MY PRINCESS

My Princess, Sweet Princess
Let down your hair,
you've been locked in a castle,
just cast away your cares.

For I am Jesus, your Lord and your Savior
I'll keep you far, far away from danger,
It began long ago when God sent me to Earth
a miraculous birth, placed away in a manger.

My love is upon you,
you know that it's true,
The greatest of love
is all over you.

Oh beautiful one,
I know your intentions,
are honest and true
of this I have mentioned
Don't think it's just you.

You prayed for your heart's desire,
a man of God,
who's filled with the passion
to go to the world
and tell them the story,
of the beautiful one who seeks out His bride.
Oh, this brings me such Glory

40 years in the Desert, you hungered and
searched,
the parched tongue of a woman left dying of
thirst.
Sandstorms, mirages, visions and dreams
Confusion and darkness now gone,
my love made you clean.

Vaya Con Dios you were once told,
you now soar with angels
and are blessed by the Lord.

The Rock of Faith

SINK OR SWIM

God has planted the seed

Will you delight in the harvest or
Will you pass it by

Will you see the light or simply let it extinguish

Be not blind to what the Lord provides for you
for He alone knows what you need

His lovely daughter has been presented to you.

Now what will you do?

DAY BY DAY

The seasons change
My heart stays true,
the truth remains,
I wait for you.

My hopeful heart seeks your face,
to ask you why that first embrace,
just felt so right, not odd or wrong,
And why, oh why, do I hear his songs?

Until you tell me to move along,
I'll listen for your true love song,
but as I wait, please give me grace
to not give up or lose my faith.

SURRENDER YOUR HEART

His grace is so amazing
His love forever true
That He could love me so much more
Than even I love you.

My love can be made perfect
But only through one way
To allow His love to flow through me
With my heart out of the way.

He will guide me to the light
The eternal burning flame.
I must seek His Kingdom first,
Cry out His Holy name

Anytime I feel afraid, lonely or unsure
I lift my voice, my hands, and say
Take me, I am yours!

A New Day

Every day I rise and shine
Your holy light through me
the warmth I feel
the hope I have
the grace that comes from thee.

Yesterday is no more
tomorrow not yet here
all my focus on today
With you, whom shall I fear?

Keeping my eyes open
forever looking up
knowing it is He
who always fills my cup
It overflows with blessings
ones I could not think up

Today I'm exactly where
He needs me to be
Filled with love
thanks be to God
I am finally free!

VISIONS OF LOVE

A vision appears as if by fate
I see your eyes, I know that face
I follow my heart toward a warm embrace
It seems so right, this path I take
I know not why except by faith
He has placed in me a Holy Fire
He knows my heart, my true desire

God will take me into this place
where I will know when I see his face
Let him see me for who I am
a child of God a loving woman

Filled with the spirit, aching to share
my heart's desire with His humble heir
Lord, I pray for a life of peace
down on my knees let me release
all doubts and fears not sent by you
embracing only your sweet words of truth

My Father loves me, this I know
His loving kindness tells me so
Be with me now as I leap in faith
Lift me up and give me strength
to trust in you with all my heart
That you will bless me far and apart

My hopes and dreams will rise above
all because of His vision of love

I WANT TO SEE YOU:
A SONG FOR MY SAVIOR

I want to see you in the morning
I want to see you in the night
I want to see you in the sunshine
I want to see you in the moonlight
I love you, my Savior, and I never want to part,
'cause I wouldn't last a day without you.

You're everything I've hoped for
You're my comforter and healer
you're the dark turned into light
you're the peace that calms my spirit
you're the only thing that's right
I love you, my Lord, and I never want to part,
'cause I wouldn't last a day without you.

You're everything I've dreamed of
You're the one who hears my longings
you're the one who knows my strife
you're the one who gives me wisdom,
you're the one who holds me tight.
I love you, my Savior, and I never want to part,
'cause I wouldn't last a day without you.

You're all I've ever needed
You're the Alpha and Omega

You're my Father and my friend
You're yesterday, today, tomorrow
The beginning and the end.
I love you, my Jesus, and I never want to part,
'cause I wouldn't last a day without you.

I want to see you in the morning
I want to see you in the night
I want to see you in the sunshine
I want to see you in the moonlight
I love you, my Savior, and I never want to part,
'cause I wouldn't last a day without you.

FAMILIAR STRANGER

I have a feeling deep inside
It makes no sense in others' eyes.
Seems unreal, too good to be true,
but something tells me, it could be you.

A woman who was trapped by lies,
now reaches out, you by her side.
A stranger, yet not strange at all,
ever since He made the call,
I've felt things falling into place.
No more shame, no more disgrace.

A second chance, or is it a third,
who's counting now, it seems absurd.
The past is past, I search for truth,
Love, happiness with my new birth.

I know the love I've found in you,
the kind that's perfect and oh, so true.
Lord, let me seek you for my true love,
In peace, hope and faith in God above.

MY FATHER'S LOVE

How is it you know me so well
My heart, my soul, my spirit, my mind.

I cried out, you taught me to trust
to praise you through it all
never losing faith in you.

Your loving kindness fills me
with peace, a restored faith
stronger than yesterday
toward even brighter tomorrows.

This walk will not be easy,
but it's all I know
all I want
all I ever need.

Receiving God's Strength

NEW LIFE, NEW LIGHT

The world is so very different now
I see things through your eyes
My vision clear
I now see truth and lies

He uses me to share my story
questions of how and why
They reach to me for comfort
I hear their silent cries

I know it is not me they see,
But the Spirit who lives inside
I am honored by your presence
Oh, My Lord, you are divine

Please make yourself at home in me
I've cleared out lots of space
for now I know that all is well
since I met you in this place

OUTER SHELL

I am God's creation
Without a shadow of a doubt
through the miracle of birth,
I entered with a shout.

Oh, Lord, the innocence and hope
that you instilled at birth,
How did I lose it, let it slip away
rob me of my youth?

I lost such precious minutes, hours, days and
years,
I let my deepest darkest doubts envelope me with
fear.

But your mercy, it endures
You told me I am yours
There's nothing I can do or say
To lose your love that cures.

The vessel you created many years ago,
I only showed the outer shell,
My true self yet to show.

I kept myself hidden deep inside
Locked up and sealed tight
Threw away the key and numbed my heart

Yet your love told me to fight.
To show them who I really am
All you say, it's true
Each day my purpose and my goal
Is to live my life for you.

I CRY OUT

Today the darkness gave me his best shot
He launched fiery darts of doubt
and fear straight at
my heart.

But he is no match for thee.
The strength of You is forever within me.

LED

Lead me down the narrow road
toward the junction with a kindred soul.
The fog will lift, the static clear
I hear your voice whisper in my ear.

I see your face, your presence near.
My soul does surge, the time is here .
Long suffering I've withstood
to learn my life could be so good.

I'm meant for love, compassion, truth,
not long, cold days so far from you.
Not lonely days on end, I'm meant for love
with my husband and my friend.

I searched and fought to make life right.
Not knowing the missing piece of my life.
My heart was numb, shielded from pain,
you held me close while the truth remained.

I needed you to show me how
to love others, in your way now.
You teach me every single day
to let go of me and live your way.

It's not a choice of yes or no,
there is no turning back, no stop or go.

You've filled me with a new desire
to live, to love, to spread the fire.

I stand for you, by your word so true,
it's you and me, for me it's you.

A BIRTHDAY WISH FOR MY DAD

I search for words to explain
exactly how I feel
to let you know how much I care,
my love for you is so real

Sometimes I struggle with the words
I cannot find my voice
so this poem I write to you
it is my heartfelt choice

Many years ago, you chose me
and I realize today
how fortunate I really am
to be loved in such a special way

Although the miles separate us
we're never far apart
I wish you Happy Birthday, Dad
from the bottom of my heart

WITH LOVING THANKS TO:

Without the inspiration, love and encouragement of these individuals, this book would not have been possible:

My Heavenly Father, My Lord and Savior, Jesus Christ for restoring my childlike faith and igniting the desire to share the stories of my heart.

My Son, Stephen, for the love, faith, and laughter we share, you are truly a blessing from above.

Dad and Vy, Libby and family, Scott and family, Melissa and family and of course you Mom...I feel you smiling down on me from Heaven!

My birth parents, for having the courage and strength to let me go into God's trusting hands.

Dinah, Dolores and my Thursday night sisters, Linda, Danny, Chris, Ruth, Abbie, Cheryl, Diane, Chrisanne, Julie, Patrick, Eric & Leslie, Joyce Meyer, Special K and Patty.

Special thanks to:

Pastor Kenny Foreman, Pastor Ken Foreman, Pastor Mike Garcia, Pastor Rose Gomez and the entire Cathedral of Faith Family.

The CSN family for helping me bring my vision to completion.